WALLET SHARE

Tammy —

All the best to
one of the best!

Wallet Share

Grow Your Practice Without Adding Clients

>>> L.Harris
Partners

LEE EISENSTAEDT, MBA
TOM SIDERS, CPA, CGMA

NOTICE TO READERS
Wallet Share: Grow Your Practice Without Adding Clients
is distributed with the understanding that the authors and
publisher are not rendering legal, accounting or other professional services in the publication. If legal advice or other expert
assistance is required, the services of a competent professional
should be sought.

Special discounts on bulk quantities of this book are available
to professional associations, corporations, and other organizations. For details, contact info@LHarrisPartners.com or call
(952) 944-3303.

Wallet Share:
Grow Your Practice Without Adding Clients
Copyright © 2013 by Lee H. Eisenstaedt and Thomas R. Siders

All rights reserved. Except as permitted under U.S. Copyright
Act of 1976, no part of this publication may be reproduced,
distributed, or transmitted in any form or by any means, or
stored in a database or retrieval system, without the prior
written permission of the authors.

ISBN: 978-1482771138

Publisher: CreateSpace Independent Publishing Platform
Marketing Advisors: Tami Wendt and Amanda Isaacson
Cover Design and Illustration: Stephan Chobanian
Interior illustrations: Tami Wendt
Interior Design and Typography: Stephan Chobanian
Editor: Brett Prytle

Visit our website at www.LHarrisPartners.com

Acknowledgements

We must first thank Jeff Johnson and Chad Koebnick, our partners in the business, who listened to us and offered valuable insight and counsel. While their names are not on the cover, their contributions made this book possible. We also thank our marketing advisors, Tami Wendt and Amanda Isaacson, for their understanding and guidance throughout this project.

We are also grateful to our consulting clients and attendees of our presentations at various conferences and workshops, as they have served as sounding boards, shared their experiences with us, and helped us refine our ideas.

Last, but not least, our thanks goes to the thousands of clients of professional service firms who respond to our surveys annually, providing us with valuable insights about their needs and how they want to be served by their accountants and other professional advisors.

Contents

Background xi

Chapter 1
Client Prioritization 1

Chapter 2
Change Behaviors and Results by
Understanding the Client's Reality 11

Chapter 3
Why Did That Client Leave? 27

Chapter 4
3x3x3℠ Client Service Model 37

Chapter 5
3x3x3℠ Client Service Plans 49

Chapter 6
3x3x3℠ Accountability 63

Chapter 7
Building On the 3x3x3℠ Model 73

Closing Thoughts 85

About L. Harris Partners 88

LEE H. EISENSTAEDT, MBA

Lee Eisenstaedt brings more than 35 years of finance and operations experience to the clients of L. Harris Partners, who benefit from his unique ability to understand both sides of the client-service equation.

Since co-founding L. Harris Partners, LLC in 2010, Lee's engagements have included serving as the Chief of Operations for a top 50 accounting firm and surveying/interviewing several thousand clients of professional services firms. Prior to L. Harris Partners, Lee served as Chief Operating Officer for the Upper Midwest region of a top five national accounting firm. Before that time, he spent 21 years with the SC Johnson family of companies – including the consumer products company, the SC Johnson family office, and Johnson Outdoors, Inc. – in the U.S. and Western Europe. Lee also spent six years with Baxter International, Inc. in finance and accounting positions.

Lee is a frequent speaker at national and regional conferences of practitioners of professional services including the American Institute of Certified Public Accountants (AICPA), Association for Accounting Marketing, Legal Marketing Association, and Moore Stephens North America.

Lee received his MBA from Northwestern University and his BA from Franklin & Marshall College. He has attended executive programs on marketing at Harvard, Wharton, and Northwestern Universities, and is a member of the Association for Accounting Marketing, and an associate member of the AICPA, and the Illinois Society of CPAs.

About the Authors

Thomas R. Siders, cpa, cgma

Tom Siders has a 35-year history of successfully managing professional services practices of all sizes. His expertise spans industries and practice areas, with a particular focus on client growth and client retention programs, practice diagnostics, firm operations and strategy development.

Prior to co-founding L. Harris Partners, LLC in 2010, Tom was an executive at a top five national accounting firm. In that role, he had responsibility for several national niche services and geographic practices, with combined revenue in excess of $350 million. He redesigned the firm's business planning process, led the development and launch of the firm's federal government practice, and was responsible for the firm's wealth advisory and broker-dealer business.

As a practicing CPA, Tom was a recognized leader in his field. He was called upon to provide expert testimony before a Joint Taxation Subcommittee of the Iowa legislature regarding the impact of Iowa's tax policies on closely held manufacturers. He has also served on the AICPA's Assurance Services Committee.

Tom received his BA degree from the University of Iowa.

The Wallet Share Process

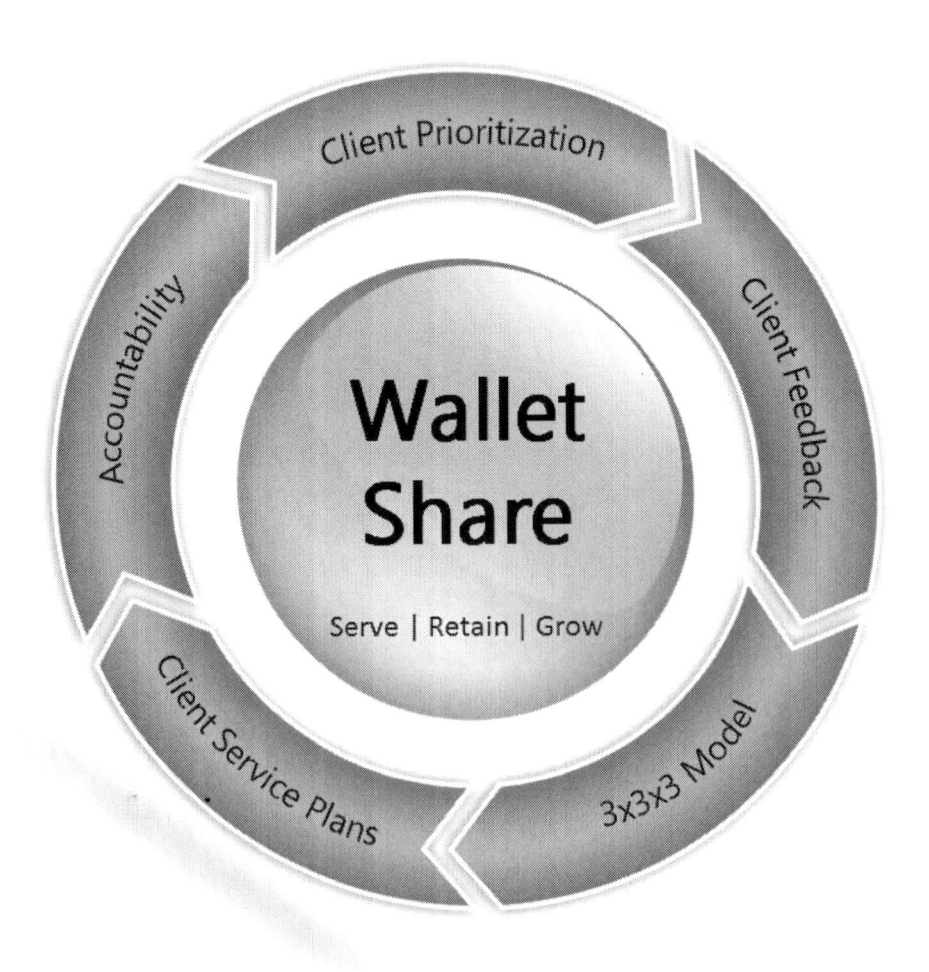

Wallet Share

Serve | Retain | Grow

- Client Prioritization
- Client Feedback
- 3x3x3 Model
- Client Service Plans
- Accountability

Background

*"Excellent firms don't believe in excellence
—only in constant improvement and constant change."*
—*Tom Peters*

This book is based on our first-hand learnings and experience as practitioners, clients and members of CPA firm management during turbulent economic times. Those vantage points have done much to shape our perspective, as leaders accountable for both building businesses and for helping others set and meet their growth and profitability objectives.

Do not presume from the subtitle of the book that we recommend you stop adding new clients. New clients are critical to every practice. But, we are convinced that practitioners do not fully capture the significant incremental revenue inherent in their current client base.

Like most practitioners, we had been serving our clients for a long time. We knew their industries, businesses and, quite frequently, their families. We believed that the keys to retaining clients and growing the business through referrals were providing great service and doing excellent work. We were confident that our clients knew us, liked us and trusted us, and that we knew what was best for them.

However, that seemingly comfortable world began to change in two distinct waves, the first of which began in about 2003. That's when:

- The Enron debacle led to the passage of Sarbanes Oxley, dramatically increasing the demand for accounting services.

- All accounting and tax service professionals could be rainmakers if they knew how to answer the phone.

- There was precious little time to focus on current clients because partners were too busy onboarding new clients.

- The war for talent was not winnable because there was not enough supply of talented people in financial services.

The second—and much more destructive wave came in 2008. That's when:

- The market for accounting and tax services stopped growing.

- There was no longer a shortage of accountants.

- The Baby Boomers who were leading firms started retiring at a faster pace.

- Many firms fought to gain share from others through mergers, acquisitions and below-market pricing.

- The Internet continued to make it easier for clients to expand nationally and internationally, and to identify alternative service providers.

- It seemed that nearly all of our competitors were telling our best clients "we will love you more and charge you less." (In fairness, we were saying the same thing to their best clients, but we really meant it).

After surviving these two significant marketplace waves, we realized that doing exactly what we had done before wasn't going to get us where we wanted to go. We couldn't even think of another thriving business that boasted how its products, services, and solutions were substantially the same as those offered a decade ago.

Convinced that a new business model was needed, our challenge was to sell our partners on the merits of the case.

Change management in a CPA firm is difficult. In general, partners often believe the pain of change to be greater than the consequences of being complacent and satisfied with past success. Since the heyday of the early to mid-2000s, many of our partners were already earning more than they ever imagined possible. That made it that much harder to present a new business model in which we could neither guarantee they'd earn more money than today nor completely eliminate the risk they might earn less.

Faced with this challenge, we began to look at how businesses in different industries dealt with new marketplace challenges. One of our first and most significant "aha moments" occurred when we figured out that basing strategies and tactics solely on what we thought our clients needed was both arrogant and unsustainable. By taking this insular approach, it was likely that we would miss major market shifts and fail to capitalize on a range of larger opportunities with existing clients. Worse yet, many of those overlooked opportunities tended to have better margins and were more highly valued by clients.

In order to successfully start building more of an "outside in" model, we started to adopt practices used by successful consumer products companies and financial institutions. Among other things, that meant creating and adopting structured, repeatable tools and processes to learn more about what our clients thought. This included:

- Collecting feedback that was data-driven, objective and focused on key client elements, such as why they retained us in the first place, what they actually valued in our services, and why they elected to stay with us for the long term.

- Gathering feedback through a combination of face-to-face meetings and electronic surveys. Having individuals unrelated to the clients collect and interpret all client feedback minimized the potential for bias in the results.

- Making the insights actionable and relevant through the development of client service plans.

- Designing and using new partner and staff compensation plans, which specifically reflected the strategies and tactics that evolved from our client research.

To emphasize these points and create a catalyst for behavior changes, we started asking partners about their perceptions of what clients were experiencing. By comparing the two perspectives, we could identify specific

Perception Gaps[SM] between clients and the partners serving them, which provided further evidence that the two were not aligned.

A second key learning was realizing how much growth potential existed in our current client base. By tapping into it, and based on our experience, we found we could grow revenue by 10% or more per year for several years, without prospecting for a single new client. But to unlock this potential, we had to start valuing the expansion of services provided to existing clients in the same way we valued fresh business from new clients.

We needed a system to consistently prioritize clients and regularly seek their feedback so we developed the 3x3x3[SM] service model. The main focus of this model is to help ensure that clients remain "sticky," and that important relationships are maintained over the long term. We learned this can be done by delivering three services to each client, having three touch points in each client's organization, and each client having three significant touch points in your firm.

When properly applied, the 3x3x3[SM] model can effectively institutionalize the use of client service plans, which can be a great tool for holding partners and staff accountable for growing revenue from current clients. In addition to the 3x3x3[SM] model, we also started tracking our Net Promoter Score® (a measure of the likeliness of a client to refer a firm to his/her peers and colleagues) and Wallet Share Index℠ (how much of a client's total budget for all the services you offer that it spends with you) to monitor the overall health and growth of the business.

As the time-honored saying goes, "Experience is the best teacher." After several years of testing and refining our approach to client growth and retention, our goal in writing this book is for you to increase revenue and the value of your firm by adopting some or all of these tools. In the chapters that follow, we'll explain each of them and share real examples of how they've been used.

Good luck! We also invite you to share your experiences with these tools and processes with other practitioners on the Web at www.MoreWalletShare.com.

Lee Eisenstaedt (Chicago, 312.775.4055)
Tom Siders (Minneapolis, 952.944.3303)
www.LHarrisPartners.com

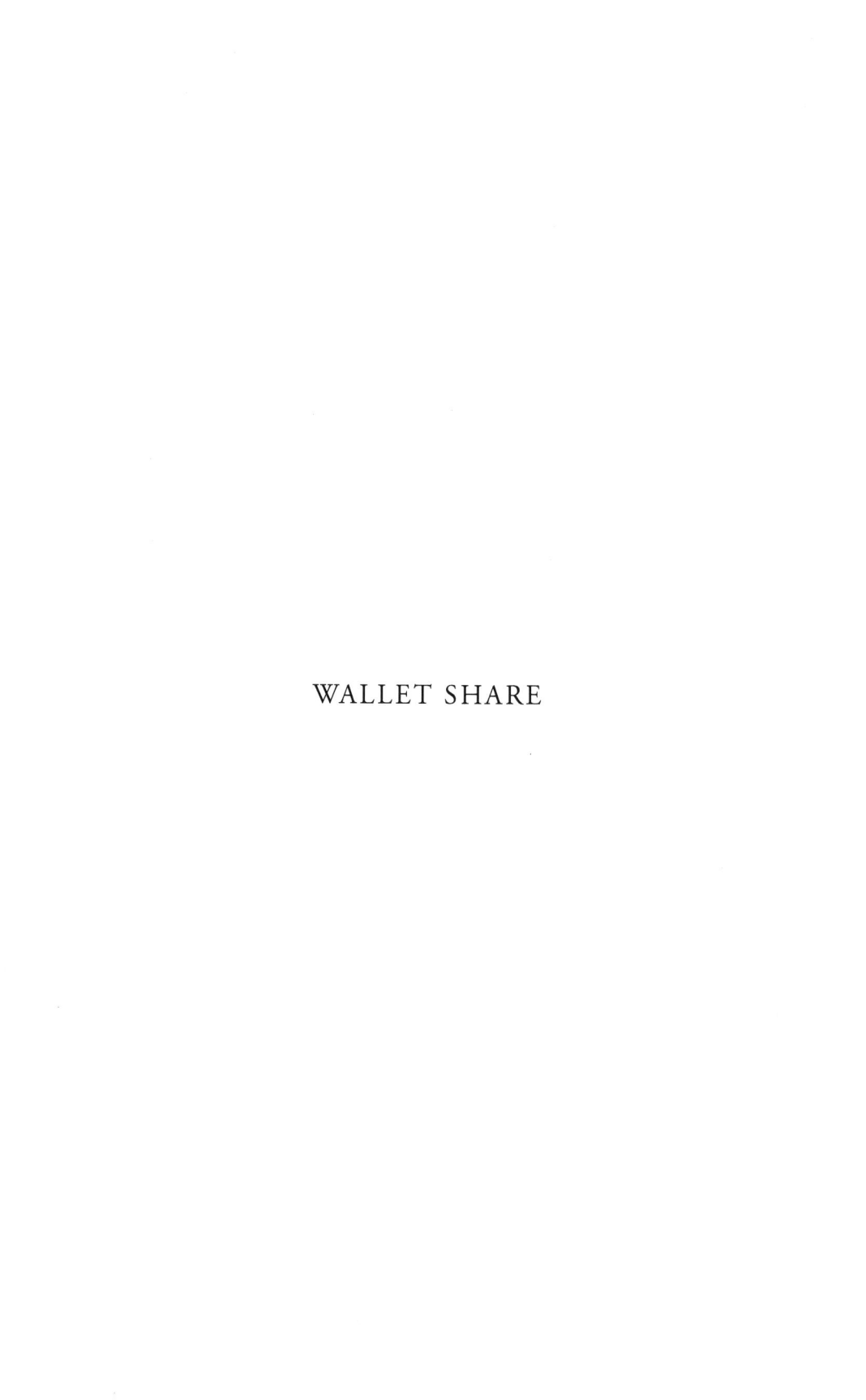

WALLET SHARE

CHAPTER 1

Client Prioritization

*"It is not enough to be busy, so are the ants.
The question is, 'What are we busy about?'"*
—*Henry David Thoreau*

Creating a client prioritization system for your firm is an essential first step in retaining loyal clients and mining incremental revenue from your current client base. While a firm's current client base is usually the quickest and most cost effective source of revenue growth, our annual surveys of accounting firms over the past four years show that more than half do not understand the amount or nature of potential untapped revenue. Additionally, these firms do not adequately target the right clients for those additional services.

How does this lapse occur? Most firms categorize clients using a grading system, (such as "A-B-C"), which far too often fails to consider attributes beyond annual client billings or the realization on the client's engagements. This approach is far too simplistic.

Wallet Share

Three Dimensions for Prioritizing Clients

Financial
- Annual billings
- Realization
- Realization vs. average for niche
- Rate per hour
- Payment history
- Wallet Share

Strategic
- Part of a strategic industry
- Expansion potential
- Number of services used
- Advisory vs. compliance
- Risk of client/engagement

Client
- Impact on firm's processes
- Marquee client
- Source of referrals
- Amount of "maintenance" required
- Effect on staff morale
- Length of relationship

A credible and convincing prioritization system considers not only historical financial metrics (such as the firm's billings to the client), but an estimate of the client's total spend on "CPA-type services," such as auditing, bookkeeping, tax or consulting work. It should also consider how many services a client uses, with more weight given to advisory than compliance services. Firms should determine a client's typical annual spend, the firm's share of that annual spend (also known as Wallet Share) and determine how that data should affect the client's overall classification.

The client's average annual spend is an example of a financial attribute that we characterize as the first of three dimensions of client prioritization.

In addition to a client's willingness to purchase services and related financial considerations, the second dimension of prioritization is strategic fit, which considers the client's industry niche, importance to the firm and overall risk.

Issues of strategic fit should not be overlooked. For example, are your top-priority clients in industry niches that your firm is well qualified to serve? If you serve only one client in a given industry, how knowledgeable is your firm about that marketplace and how well can your firm deliver the unique service offerings clients in that industry demand? Consider this rule of thumb: For a niche market to be sustainable within a firm, workflow should require at least three full-time staff.

Risk is also important to strategic fit. If your firm does not understand a specific industry, why take on significant financial and reputation risk to serve one client in that market niche?

Recently, we witnessed a discussion between two partners that helps illustrate the point. The firm had a client who needed an international transfer pricing study done to facilitate inter-company business activity between its subsidiaries in Western Europe and a manufacturing center in Italy. The firm's consulting leader was very eager to take on the project, but the partner in charge of tax argued the firm lacked the expertise to handle the study. On closer inspection, it turned out the consulting leader's confidence in handling this complex project was rooted in just one such study his group had previously conducted. While this story had a happy ending (the firm referred the engagement to a specialty tax practice with which they had an alliance), in a majority of similar cases a firm accepts the work, thus exposing its client and itself to significant risk.

Here's another example. Assume your firm has a concentration of clients in the distribution industry. Two clients in this niche are classified as "A" (or top priority) clients by your firm, based on annual billing, and both use your firm for audit and tax preparation services. The annual billing to each of these clients is $100,000. However, both are struggling financially, and both are routinely out of compliance with bank covenants. One is in danger of losing bank financing. Meanwhile, the other is actively seeking a buyer, and is adamant that their financials must justify the higher sales price they are seeking. Another client in this industry niche only uses your firm for business valuation services and spends, on average, $10,000 annually with your firm. As a result, this client is classified as a "C."

But by digging deeper into each of these situations, you discover the following circumstances. The two "A" clients rarely buy consulting or planning services from your firm, and a review of their general ledger indicates they rarely engage any outside consultants for value-added services. Neither "A" client has ever referred a potential new account to your firm. On the other hand, your "C" client is growing at 15% per year, is actively seeking acquisition targets and spends nearly $300,000 annually on audit, tax, planning, and consulting services. Those services are currently spread between your firm and three competitors. The "C" client has been very complimentary of your firm's business valuation expertise, and has referred two new prospects to your firm for similar services in the past 12 months.

While the firm should continue providing the two $100,000 clients with good service, the growth potential of those relationships is limited. Conversely, the "C" client finds value in the limited slice of services you provide, has been a referral source, is growing rapidly and is a big buyer of professional services. In our prioritization model, this account is the real "A" client for your firm, due to its significant growth potential. In later chapters, we will discuss specific steps that can help you secure more work from these "high-potential" clients.

The third dimension of a solid prioritization system is client characteristics. These traits are unique to each client, and include a willingness to make referrals or to be a reference for your firm, the length of the relationship, the working relationship between the client and your staff, the client's impact on your firm's service model, and the level of maintenance required to keep the client satisfied.

While all of these traits are important, the impact of client behavior on your staff is perhaps the most critical element. Simply put, staff turnover is expensive. Studies routinely claim the cost of staff turnover is at least double or triple the employee's annual compensation when measured by lost productivity, recruiting expense and the cost of training replacement staff.

Client Prioritization

In our experience, "clients behaving badly" causes more staff turnover than "partners behaving badly." Consider the following example: One of your partners serves three large "A-list" clients, based on annual billings. Two of the clients are in a "sweet spot" industry niche for your firm, and the interactions between your employees and client staff are positive, productive and professional. As a result, spots on these accounts are highly coveted assignments within your firm.

Meanwhile, the third client is your firm's largest account, but the only client served in a specific industry. This client is disorganized and demanding, and the overall relationship is dysfunctional. Due to this "badge of courage" assignment, all in-charge accountants and client managers assigned to this client over the last three years have left your firm for competitors within three months of completing the annual engagement.

Does our example sound outrageous? Sadly, based on our experience, it is not. When abusive clients are also classified as "A" clients, consider that your best staff is often assigned to meet their every need. Regardless of the billings, that's a losing proposition. If bad clients drive the best and brightest out of our firms, we all lose.

As you can see, the financial, strategic and client characteristics dimensions need to be viewed as an integrated package when prioritizing existing accounts. To accomplish this goal, your firm needs to recast its vision of "best clients" by applying a consistent definition of A, B & C categories. This includes billings, the client's wallet and potential to gain a larger share of it, the ability to cross-sell, whether the industry niche is right for your firm, and the impact of client behavior on your staff.

Firm management needs to take the lead in categorizing clients. The results should be shared and reviewed with each partner and adjustments made based on their input. The final results of client prioritization should drive the staffing of client engagements, meaning that your best staff should be assigned to the real "A" clients. They should also define the list of clients selected for client service plans, a topic covered in a later chapter.

Once the new client prioritization list is in place, it can be integrated into several of your firm's processes. These include, but are not limited to, scheduling, new client prospecting, new client intake (client acceptance), current client re-evaluation and retention, pricing and managing of write-offs and write-downs.

Key Learnings

- Ensure your best clients are getting the best service by prioritizing accounts on a regular basis.

- Use a multi-dimensional model to prioritize clients. This model should include key attributes, such as financial impact, strategic fit and client characteristics.

- Apply the multi-dimensional model across the firm to achieve objective results. Note that factors in the model must be adjusted to reflect differences among business practices (e.g., realization between a manufacturer and a not-for-profit agency can be substantial).

- The client prioritization ranking is only a starting point for a more detailed conversation. Prioritizing clients will take 80% of emotion and subjective issues out of the discussion, but leaves ample room for management judgment and discretion.

Wallet Share Ideas to Try in Our Firm

Barriers to Implementation

Chapter 2

Change Behaviors and Results by Understanding the Client's Reality

"I'm willing to tell ya. I'm wanting to tell ya. I'm waiting to tell ya."—Alfred P. Doolittle (character) from "My Fair Lady" (1964)

Let's start with a troubling series of mistaken perceptions:

- 51% of CPA firm leaders believe they lose clients or competitive bids because of fees, while only 25% believe they win competitive bids because they are the low-cost provider. (L. Harris Partners' 2013 Growth Prospects Survey)

- 60 to 80% of clients will tell you they are satisfied or very satisfied, right up to the day they leave. (BusinessWeek, October 2006)

- 80% of business leaders believe they are providing a superior client experience while only 8% of their clients share this feeling (Bain & Company's "Customer Led Growth" diagnostic questionnaire).

- 73% of CPA firm leaders believe their clients are receiving good service, while just 34% of clients feel they are getting good service (Jean Caragher, Capstone Consulting, 2011)

- 87% of CPA firm leaders believe their clients will refer them to new business opportunities, while only 23% of their clients say they are willing to make those referrals (Jean Caragher, Capstone Consulting, 2011)

- 96% of accounting firm leaders claim they need to improve their firm's skill at cross-selling services to clients (L. Harris Partners' 2013 Growth Prospects Survey)

We hope you'll agree that there are Perception Gaps[SM] between CPA firms and their clients. We have yet to conduct a client assessment for a CPA firm in which such gaps do not exist and where the partners were not surprised by much of what we uncovered. For example, we have found that more than 40% of business clients use multiple CPA firms, which typically comes as "news" to these firms.

These sorts of "surprises" should not come as a shock. Our research shows that 59% of CPA firm leaders believe they don't spend nearly enough time understanding the unmet and emerging needs of their clients and prospects.

When we survey clients of professional service firms, we ask about additional services they would like their firm to offer. It's common for the feedback to include services the firm already provides. In one of our engagements to survey clients of a law firm, several responded that they wanted the firm to add intellectual property to its menu of services. It was a good idea, but the firm already had such a practice and it was one of its top five revenue generators. Similarly, several clients of a CPA firm suggested the firm offer wealth management, which was already one of the firm's marquee offerings.

What happens when firms pay closer attention to closing Perception Gaps? Our experience shows this process can lead to:

- Clearer insight into client service preferences (e.g., expected response times to questions, phone calls, and email).

- Better identification of referral sources.

- Stronger understanding of unmet and emerging client needs.

- More accurate knowledge of why clients use you and your firm's competitors.

- Proactive strengthening and/or salvaging key relationships.

- Greater opportunities for additional work previously unknown to the firm.

- Increased client loyalty and retention.

- Faster growth in wallet share, revenue, profitability and partner compensation.

IDENTIFYING PERCEPTION GAPS

What's the best prescription for pinpointing if, or where, Perception Gaps exist? It's simple: Listen to your clients. Remember, this isn't about selling, entertaining or deal making. This is about taking the time to ask good questions, carefully listening to clients' answers and learning from their wisdom.

To get the right insights from the right people, you need a structured, disciplined, repeatable process composed of multiple feedback loops. This can include:

- *Top-to-Top meetings:* This involves ad-hoc, face-to-face relationship building meetings between the client and the firm's top executive(s).

- *Post-engagement satisfaction surveys:* This often consists of electronic or phone surveys that are driven by events, such as the end of an engagement or a call to the Help Desk. These surveys are designed to understand how an experience compares with the client's expectations.

- *Periodic assessments:* By using e-surveys and face-to-face meetings, you can assess how receptive your clients are to competitors' advances, gauge their awareness of your brand, and/or measure the degree of engagement with your staff.

- *Snapshot assessments:* This tool involves deep dives into strategic segments of a business, and it's typically done via face-to-face meetings or over the phone.

Tools like SurveyMonkey® (www.SurveyMonkey.com) and Constant Contact® (www.ConstantContact.com) make it easy for firms to send professional, electronic surveys to their clients. Here are a few important tips to keep in mind when designing them:

> **Tips for Improving Survey Response Rates**
>
> ☑ Keep it short. The best response rates come from surveys under five minutes. (Test the duration to confirm the timing.)
>
> ☑ Tell invitees up front how long the survey will take.
>
> ☑ Send surveys on a Tuesday or Wednesday.
>
> ☑ Keep questions simple. Avoid asking multiple things in the same question (e.g. "I am satisfied with the team assigned to my account and our fees").
>
> ☑ Hold surveys open for no more than two weeks.
>
> ☑ Send out reminders to encourage completion.

Face-to-face and phone interviews should be conducted by two people whenever possible. Why? Because we all listen and interpret things differently. It's like each of us is a radio tuned to a different station. Differences in what each person heard about a client's plans, needs, and expectations for innovation, quality and service should be identified and reconciled during a post-interview de-brief.

EXPERIENCE THE WISDOM OF CLIENTS

In addition, our experience shows that including a partner in client interviews is key to accelerating behavioral and culture change. Early on, we met alone with clients before faithfully reporting back to partners on what we heard. We found that the partners mostly looked engaged, but did not truly understand the nuances of or bought into what we had learned. That quickly changed when we started to take partners on interviews to experience first-hand the wisdom of our clients.

For this approach to be effective, the partner must not be involved with the client. His/her role in the meeting must be carefully crafted, and we have had the best success when a partner's role is limited to asking the client a series of quantitative questions. This requires good preparation and coaching so the partner does not get defensive and resists the temptation to dwell on sensitive tactical issues (such as pricing, policies, etc.) that may arise.

Using third-party interviewers for face-to-face and phone interviews is highly recommended. It will cost a bit more, but clients are more likely to give the most candid and direct responses to questions asked by people unrelated to the engagement. Interviewers can be retired partners, your marketing director or trained professionals from outside the firm. The latter are particularly effective when they have firsthand experience as client servers and/or clients of professional services firms. Regardless of their background, the most important characteristics of good interviewers are experience, the ability to ask sound, focused questions, and the patience to be an active listener.

IMPROVE YOUR RANKING

When firms hit a barrier in their efforts to improve client satisfaction, it's helpful to understand where the firm ranks relative to its competitors and how your firm compares to their concept of the ideal accounting, tax, and consulting firm. For example, determining what competitors are doing that compels a client to prefer them to you is a critical client learning. To gain insight on such a question, consider using an electronic survey of a targeted client base.

What do you have to gain from gauging competitive rankings? Consider the following example. Many of us are "satisfied" with Wal-Mart, Kmart and Target. However, we generally have a preference for one of them, for example, Target. If Wal-Mart and Kmart understood what causes us to rank Target as our top choice, they would have valid insights about what they have do to improve their ranking. That improvement, in turn, may lead to us spending more of our budget with Wal-Mart and/or Kmart. (Harvard Business Review, *Customer Loyalty Isn't Enough. Grow Your Share of Wallet*, October 2012).

ASSESSING CLIENT LOYALTY AND VULNERABILITY
In addition to competitor research, another tool we have found effective at accelerating behavior change is a "full circle" perception assessment. This means gathering the perceptions of clients by partners at the same time as you gather perceptions of clients about the firm. We do this as part of our Vulnerability Matrix[SM], which assesses a client's vulnerability to the advances of competitors by asking four questions:

- How likely is the client to refer the firm onto others? (i.e., the Net Promoter Score)

- Are the services provided by the firm a good value?

- Is the firm easy to work with?

- Is the firm capable of meeting the client's needs for the next 2-4 years?

We then ask the partners serving those clients how each of them believes their client(s) answered those four questions. When the responses of the partners and their clients are compared, Perception Gaps are generally exposed.

Our surveys of partners frequently find they underrate their performance and that the most commonly downplayed attribute is the client's likelihood to refer the firm to others. We regularly find in our surveys of clients of CPA firms that 60% to 75% of them are willing to refer their CPA firm onto others. Between 65% and 80% of them have actually made a referral. But, about half of the clients will only make a referral when prompted to do so, and we find that just 20% to 35% of CPAs have asked their clients for referrals.

The key learning is that if you don't think you'll get a referral, the likelihood is low that you'll ask for one. Clearly, not asking for a referral is the top reason for not getting one.

WHEN TO SEEK FEEDBACK

There's never a bad time to invest in client feedback and retention (unless, of course, it's after a key client leaves). The best time to seek feedback is when clients are actually using your services. For most CPA firms, this means February through April. Here's why:

- It's your busy season, not your clients'. Most clients aren't under the same pressures from February through April as you. They will most likely have time to meet with representatives of your firm (and competitors as well).

- Your weaknesses are exposed. During your busy season, your clients are experiencing your services when they are stretched to their design limits. Weaknesses and cracks in the foundation may begin to appear. Proactively asking for feedback during busy season will allow you to identify key issues and fix them before they become major problems.

- You've got their attention. Clients are more aware of your services when they're in the middle of using them. This makes February through April the perfect time to engage them in meaningful conversations. This process allows you to reconfirm what's most important to them and demonstrate how much you value the relationship.

- Not everyone is tied up with work. Not everyone within your firm is consumed with serving clients during busy season. It's likely your marketing director, chief financial officer or the partner leading your consulting practice can find time to visit top clients from February through April.

- The process can be outsourced. Most client feedback initiatives can be outsourced without compromising quality. Using an independent third party reduces positive bias and frees up time of partners and staff for client service and billable hours. Engaging outside expertise also demonstrates to your clients that you value building a high-quality relationship with them.

- Clients may feel ignored. Multiple research studies have shown that about two-thirds of clients leave their CPA firm because they feel ignored or taken for granted. From February through April, your focus is probably fixed on getting your clients' work completed and meeting deadlines you cannot move. As a result, you run the risk of missing important cues from key clients that make them feel disconnected from your firm.

Who To Ask?

In addition to choosing a time frame for client feedback, the second most asked question we receive from our clients is "who" to approach. While the answer depends on what you're trying to understand, here's whom we frequently suggest:

- The 20% of clients that account for 80% of revenue.

- The firm's most and least profitable clients.

- Clients within a strategic industry or niche.

- Clients who utilize multiple services and can be benchmarked against a sample of clients who use just one service.

- Clients who have been with the firm for one year, who can be benchmarked against a sample of clients who have been with the firm for five, seven, or ten years.

As a general rule, it's wise to seek feedback from more than one person at each client organization (whenever possible). Don't just ask questions of the CFO or CEO. Ask questions of a broader cut of staff directly involved with the client relationship. Why? Because while one of these people may be a raving fan, it may not be the case throughout the organization. You need to identify detractors because, over time, they can severely damage the relationship. Conversely, don't just ask your firm's relationship partner for his or her client perceptions. Ask other partners and staff assigned to the engagement about their thoughts on the relationship.

We regularly see significant differences between the Audit and Tax partners regarding the same client. We've also seen first and second generations of family-owned businesses not share the same opinions of their accountants, lawyers, and investment advisors. And, it's common for staff to have very different experiences with your firm or a client's organization than your firm's partners or the client's CEO or CFO.

How Often To Solicit Feedback?

Another frequent question we get is "how often" to solicit feedback. While that also depends on the objective, here are some guidelines to use as a starting point:

Type of Assessment	Which Clients to Ask	When to Ask	Preferred Way to solicit Feedback	Interviewer
Pre-engagement assessment of how the client will judge the firm and team	All engagements over a minimum size (e.g. $10,000 per year)	Beginning of new relationship	Face-to-face or telephone	In-sourced
Top to top meeting	Top 10-20 clients for the firm, a practice, an office, etc.	Annually	Face-to-face or telephone	In-sourced
Survey of client satisfaction at milestones of large projects	Recurring projects and long-duration projects	Whenever milestones are reached	Electronic	In-sourced or outsourced
Post-engagement client satisfaction survey	All clients	End of Engagement	Electronic	In-sourced or outsourced
Client loyalty assessment	Top clients in the firm, a practice, an office, etc.	Every 2-3 years after baseline is established	Face-to-face, telephone or electronic	Outsourced
Survey to assess client vulnerability to advances of competitors	Broad spectrum of clients from across the firm	Annually	Electronic	Outsourced

KEY LEARNINGS
- Listening to clients helps you build stronger relationships, shift the discussion from price to value and learn about a client's strategies, priorities, risk concerns and pressure points.

- Firm leadership has to foster a culture that has a larger appetite for client insights to make day-to-day decisions.

- When we identify an "unhappy client," we face a choice about which of those two words we'll change – unhappy or client.

- Listening to clients using disciplined, structured and repeatable processes is the best way to close Perception Gaps. The more systematic the process, the more sustainable it will be.

- Soliciting feedback from clients and partners using multiple techniques leads to the best understanding of client relationships.

- To minimize positive bias, maximize honesty and optimize invested time, two people unrelated to the engagement, internal or external to the firm, should solicit feedback.

- Your busy season is one of the best times to seek client feedback.

WALLET SHARE IDEAS TO TRY IN OUR FIRM

BARRIERS TO IMPLEMENTATION

CHAPTER 3

Why Did That Client Leave?

"Your most unhappy clients are your greatest source of learning."
—Bill Gates

When a client leaves or you lose a proposal to a competitor, what do you do? We find that many firms don't do anything at all. Instead, more than half blame the loss on price and move on as if nothing had happened. We're aware of a firm that lost a $1 million client, which led to the termination of several people as the firm right-sized staffing levels to match the reduced workload. While price was blamed for the lost client, it played a minor role in client's decision to change firms.

Many of us fear honest feedback, most likely because of a bad prior experience. This could have been feedback that led to a smaller bonus, the denial of a promotion or perk, or information that was used to make us feel less valued and appreciated. When this happens, it's common to get cynical or defensive, while ignoring the important insights in that feedback.

About 18 months ago, we had a conversation with a managing partner that shouldn't have surprised us (but did). We were talking about drivers of client loyalty, which included attributes like responsiveness, continuity of the team, follow-up and follow-through. We reminded him that clients are like fingerprints and snowflakes – no two are the same – and pointed out the benefits of doing a simple client survey to understand what compelled them to retain his firm over the competition. We had been talking about this for about two hours, so we were sure he "got it."

We were mistaken. The managing partner said, "I don't think my partners would want to know what our clients think of us." Later, he added, "Come to think of it, I'm not sure I want to know either." I'm sure the expression on our faces gave us away long before one of us said: "As managing partner you're not serious." But he was. That led to another two-hour conversation to understand his fears.

In the short term, this firm chose to gather no client feedback, a choice that later came back to haunt the managing partner. About eight months after our conversation, and shortly after the toughest busy season he had experienced, he called to report he had recently lost several major clients (each of whom he had believed liked the firm's services). He wanted to know how soon we could assess a broad spectrum of his clients, so the firm could discover and address similar problems before any more clients left.

What did we take away from this conversation and others that followed with CPA firm leaders? Here's a closer look.

Feedback Phobia

A key learning from our subsequent leadership conversations is that there are many reasons why we fear seeking client feedback. Among the most common are:

Fear of the unknown. We're accustomed to knowing the answers to questions before we ask them. We like being in control of situations. When we seek feedback, we don't know what the client or prospect will say, which sends us outside our comfort zone. We open ourselves up to criticism and challenges to our judgment. On the other hand, which situation is better: Thinking you know or knowing you know?

Fear of being hammered. Many of us believe that feedback is largely negative and, when given a chance, that people will focus on our faults and weaknesses. We don't find this to be true in most cases. People are usually happy you cared enough to ask their opinion and will provide you with constructive insights. The people you need to be concerned about aren't those who rant, but those who don't tell you anything. That group typically stays silent because they don't think you care, don't believe it will change anything or feel that honesty will bring repercussions.

Fear of retribution. Some people are concerned that feedback will be reflected in performance reviews, that it will block their career progression or justify a reduction in base pay or bonus compensation. Some think HR or the Managing Partner may be using feedback to advance a secret agenda. However, we regularly see people who are open to feedback rise in organizations, often because they are perceived as better leaders.

Fear of losing control. Sometimes we fear feedback because we're unsure of how we'll react. Will we break down in tears, become defensive, get angry or say some things we don't mean? Being able to control one's emotions in these situations is among the attributes of a good leader. Carefully planning when and how feedback is delivered can help alleviate these issues.

Fear of change. Few people like change, but maintaining the status quo can be shortsighted and career limiting. Acting on feedback almost always involves some sort of change, but ignoring it is a bit like the child who covers his eyes so you can't see him. Business problems don't go away and, if left unaddressed, can worsen to the point that they can be nearly impossible to correct. That has severe consequences for the individual, team or firm.

How Can You Be So Sure?

While the items noted above may be the underlying reasons why people are reluctant to ask clients for feedback, we frequently hear other reasons for not asking clients what they think. Here are examples of the push-back we regularly receive:

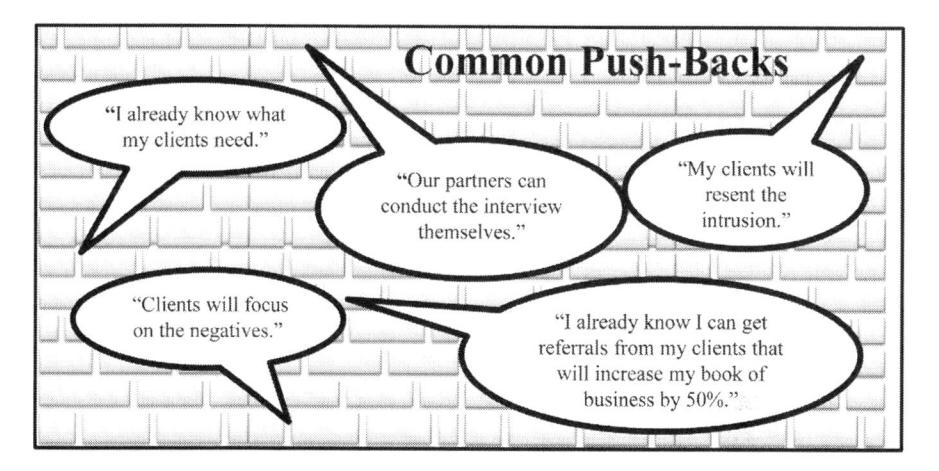

Common Push-Backs

- "I already know what my clients need."
- "Our partners can conduct the interview themselves."
- "My clients will resent the intrusion."
- "Clients will focus on the negatives."
- "I already know I can get referrals from my clients that will increase my book of business by 50%."

To better understand what's behind the objection(s), consider asking the question "How can you be so sure?" We've found that it helps separate fact from fiction, which then allows you to address the real concern(s).

Viewing Feedback as A Gift

Some people choose to treat feedback as a gift. While they'll acknowledge that feedback can be difficult to hear, many will often tell you it led to breakthrough, game-changing results. So, what can we learn from this point of view?

Feedback can reveal why the client left. We don't know what we don't know. By asking lost clients or prospects for direct and honest feedback, you can learn what could have been done differently to preserve business or add new accounts. If you're brave enough to ask, you'll find that most people will tell you what was missing and why they chose to work with someone else. They may even respect you more for asking.

As Kristen Smaby, CS Lead with Basis Science, Inc., has written on client service, "when (clients) share their story, they're not just sharing their pain points. They're actually teaching you how to make your product, service and business better."

To make clients feel comfortable providing honest feedback, consider using someone uninvolved in the engagement or proposal to solicit feedback since they bring no political or work-related biases to the feedback gathering process.

Feedback allows the client or prospect to vent and gain a sense of closure. When someone has a bad experience, they are likely to tell nine to 15 other people about it, according to the White House Office of Consumer Affairs, Washington, D.C. (unless, as Amazon's founder Jeff Bezos said, they have a bad experience on the Internet, in which case they'll tell 6,000 friends). Wouldn't you rather they tell you instead of an unpredictable number of other people? By offering unhappy clients or prospects the opportunity to share their concerns, you can help heal wounds and bad feelings (assuming you are sincere about considering changes to systems, processes and behaviors within your control). While you can't (and shouldn't) change everything, throughout the process you must keep an open mind, set aside some of your ego and demonstrate a positive attitude. Seeking this kind of feedback provides an opportunity to rebuild relationships and a chance to stay connected going forward.

Feedback provides information about competitors and their practices. Our experience shows that clients and prospects will answer just about any question you pose. But if you don't ask, it's unlikely they'll volunteer the information. Would you like to see a copy of a competitor's proposal, learn more about their pricing or determine how the job is being staffed? Ask. Would it be helpful to learn how many CPA firms the client or prospect uses, or understand what compels them to prefer their top choice to you? Ask. When you've stepped over the line, they'll tell you.

Turn Losses into Wins

While losing a client or a proposal is disappointing, there is value in the experience. By using it as a learning opportunity and coachable moment, your firm can turn those losses into wins. As Ken Blanchard, author of The One Minute Manager, once said, "Feedback is the breakfast of champions."

For example, consider tracking your firm's win/loss rate. Simply maintain a log of which proposals you win, those that are lost to a competitor and what the major factors were in deciding the outcome. Over time, this accumulated data will provide insights into what you do well and what you need to be doing differently

Another simple measure is to track the predictability of your revenue. Just count the number of clients you had last year and how many of them returned in the current year. Do the same analysis on their spending to see if the revenue remained constant, increased or declined. This simple assessment will indicate when your services are perceived as "must-haves" rather than "good-to-haves."

KEY LEARNINGS

- Seeking out feedback from lost clients and prospects is stressful and can be difficult to hear.

- Remember Stephen Covey's Sixth Habit of Highly Effective People: "Seek first to understand, then be understood."

- The feedback you receive usually provides a road-map to what needs to be changed.

- The rewards of feedback can be significant. However, it's wise to use someone who is unrelated to the bid or client to gather the information. This person can be internal to your firm or an independent third party. This approach usually helps clients feel more comfortable about providing honest input, while avoiding potentially awkward conversations.

WALLET SHARE IDEAS TO TRY IN OUR FIRM

BARRIERS TO IMPLEMENTATION

CHAPTER 4

3x3x3^{SM} Client Service Model

"The end we aim at must be known, before the way can be made."
—*Jean Paul, 1763-1825*

Have any of these scenarios ever happened to you?

- Your primary contact at a long-term client left for a new opportunity. A new CFO was hired and within a few months you lost the client to a competitor. That firm was strongly recommended by the new CFO who, it turns out, was an alumnus of that provider. Upon further review, you learn that the firm was also the primary CPA for the new CFO's last employer.

- One of your managers, on whom you rely heavily for servicing several of your larger clients, leaves to join a competitor. Your client relationships are a little dated, so you re-engage and quickly bring a new manager onto the accounts. However, due to the steep learning curve for the new manager, year-end client engagements do not go smoothly. Months later, some of these clients say they are seeking proposals from your firm and two competitors. At the end, the firm your former manager joined is awarded the work by two of these long-term clients.

- You learn that a great client has engaged a different CPA firm to provide a specialized tax service. It is a service your firm has both the expertise and capacity to perform. When you tell the client your firm could have handled the engagement and avoided the learning curve of a new provider, the client responds, "We were not aware you could handle the project. One of our suppliers referred them to us, our VP of Manufacturing heard them speak at an industry conference, and they claim to be tax experts for our industry."

If these types of situations never happen to your firm, you can skip this chapter. But do so only if your firm never loses clients, routinely surveys lost clients and knows why clients leave, or believes your firm is capturing a full share of each client's wallet.

We developed the 3x3x3[SM] model as a simple, easy-to-communicate method for helping firms create "sticky" clients and capture more wallet share. CPA firms that use this client service model create loyal, long-term clients, while not being "held hostage" by an individual partner. CPA firms that do not adopt it risk having a client base that is under-served, overly dependent on a handful of partners and highly vulnerable to competitors.

The premise of 3x3x3^{SM} is simple. For all significant clients:

- At least 3 services are delivered to the client in 3 different disciplines

- At least 3 upper level personnel have a relationship with the client

- At least 3 upper level client personnel have a relationship with the firm

The chart below illustrates the model.

3x3x3^{SM} MODEL OF CLIENT SERVICE

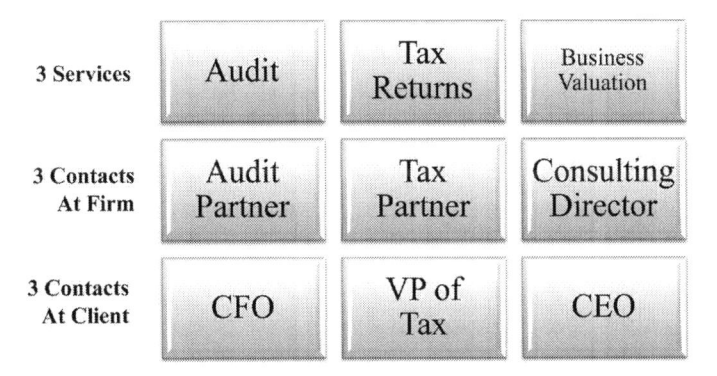

3 Services	Audit	Tax Returns	Business Valuation
3 Contacts At Firm	Audit Partner	Tax Partner	Consulting Director
3 Contacts At Client	CFO	VP of Tax	CEO

3x3x3ˢᴹ—Three Services Delivered to the Client
Research studies in various industries show that the broader the relationship between your firm and the client, the more likely you are to retain the client for the long term. For example, research in the banking industry has shown that commercial clients who purchase one financial service are likely to stay with the bank for an average of 18 months, while clients who purchase three services stay for an average of 6.8 years (Bancography, Birmingham, AL, 2010).

By implementing the 3x3x3ˢᴹ client service model, you are more likely to retain the client, survive turnover of key firm staff, and lessen relationship risks when there's turnover of vital client personnel.

According to Marketing Metrics, there's a 5 to 20% probability of successfully selling to a new prospect, but a 60 to 70% probability of successfully selling new business to an existing client. When you consider that it can be up to 11 times more expensive to secure a project from new client, the rewards for mining increased opportunities within your existing client base should be clear (The Council on Financial Competition, 2010).

So, how do you position yourself to provide at least three services to clients?

3x3x3^{SM} Client Service Model

Based on our surveys of CPA firm clients, a top attribute desired by clients is an advisor who understands their business and where they are headed. Clients want their firm to proactively bring ideas and suggestions on how to improve their business, while staying ahead of changes in their industry. Instead of generalities, clients want specific insights and advice tailored to their unique circumstances. Technical expertise is a baseline expectation. The added value comes when a firm brings unsolicited, on-target ideas and suggestions that can make a real difference in their client's overall success.

By spending time with your best clients and asking open-ended questions to really understand their goals and plans, you will discover a new palette of key needs. By doing so, you can intelligently discuss how your firm can help with a targeted range of accounting, tax, and consulting services. This may include periods and methods, cost segregation, SALT, estate and gift tax, international structuring, financial planning, technology systems, budgeting, internal controls, exit and succession planning, risk management and business valuation services.

You can download a simple one-page chart that partners can use to track, month-by-month, the touch points they have with key clients at our website, www.MoreWalletShare.com. On this chart, all of a partner's key clients are likely to fit on a single page, with activities being recorded at a level high enough to be simple, yet meaningful. Some firms have found this tool so useful that they've made it a formal part of a partner's performance review.

3x3x3^{SM}—THREE PEOPLE FROM THE FIRM
The best way to create "sticky" clients and increase wallet share is by using a team approach to serve your biggest and best clients. Those are the 20% of clients that comprise 70 to 80% of your revenue. The same holds true for smaller revenue clients with large, untapped wallet share (see Chapter 1 on prioritization).

A team is not an audit partner, audit manager, audit in-charge and a staff accountant. By team, we mean seasoned personnel from audit, tax and, if possible, consulting – even for "audit only" clients. The same concept should apply to "tax only" and "consulting only" clients. Partners who are specialty-area experts cannot possibly diagnose client issues and identify additional service opportunities across all disciplines. To successfully capture cross sell opportunities, it's important to get a full range of subject matter experts in front of the client – especially if that team has demonstrated knowledge and understanding of the client's core industry.

The team approach is more than making internal assignments or jotting down names and tossing it in the client file. It requires the primary relationship partner to open the door for broader firm involvement with the client. This involves a trust transfer process – from "client trusts the relationship partner" to "client trusts the firm." By expanding the relationship from a single partner to a team of at least three senior firm personnel, your client is much more likely to understand the breadth and depth of your service capabilities. It will also bolster the client's confidence that the business relationship with your firm is highly valued and reinforce how they made a good choice when they selected your firm.

If your firm is not large enough to form a multi-disciplined team, we suggest you form an alliance with a specialty consulting firm that can help fill in any specific talent gaps. An alliance can broaden your firm's service offerings and make your firm capable of handling more diverse client needs without worrying about competition for your core service lines. While many potential strategic partners clearly wish to form alliances with CPA firms because of the new business opportunities such a deal represents, note that the best alliances are those where your alliance partner is also referring business to you.

3x3x3^{SM}—Three Members of Client Management
Your business relationship is at risk if you have just one connection within the client's management team, even if that relationship is with a 100% owner. Other

members of client management are influencers who can support or undermine relationships with key decision makers. They can also influence decisions about who to hire for special projects. Our work surveying former clients who left for new service providers confirms that relying on a single point-of-contact at the clients puts the relationship at risk.

By moving from a single relationship partner to a multi-disciplined client service team, your firm can triple the odds it will be "top-of-mind" for new engagement opportunities. And, by expanding your client relationships with multiple members of the management team, the opportunity to raise awareness of your firm's capabilities expands geometrically.

For example, if your client is nearing retirement, is leading a privately held company or uses your wealth management services, then it's smart to build connections with his/her spouse, children and other trusted advisors. Building these relationships will help reduce the likelihood that you are replaced when the next generation of the family assumes control of the business and other assets, such as trusts.

The client retention benefit of 3x3x3^{SM} should be obvious. By developing three connections within your firm and three strong connections at the client, you have a much greater "emotional" connection that can survive common turnover and succession issues. In addition, the 3x3x3℠ approach positions your firm to provide multiple client services, because your team can understand and assess the client's goals, plans and needs from different points of view. Providing the client with multiple services, beyond just audit and tax compliance, is also more profitable and makes switching firms much more complicated.

Bottom-line: When a client feels like they are attached to your firm, and not just a particular partner, it's very likely that client will become "sticky."

KEY LEARNINGS

- To create a sticky client, your firm needs to develop three upper-level client relationships, the client needs to have three upper-level partner relationships and the client needs to be using at least three of your services.

- We call this the 3x3x3[SM] model for client service. It drives client retention, firm loyalty, and increases in wallet share. These, in turn, lead to revenue growth, greater profitability, and more funds to invest in the business or increase partner compensation.

- If your client is nearing retirement, building relationships with key family members and trusted advisors should be part of that client's 3x3x3[SM] model.

Wallet Share Ideas to Try in Our Firm

Barriers to Implementation

CHAPTER 5

3x3x3[SM] Client Service Plans

"A goal without a plan is just a wish."
—*Antoine de Saint-Exupéry*

We have found that leaders of CPA firms quickly grasp the concept of the 3x3x3[SM] Model for serving, retaining and growing clients.

But, introducing the concept in ways that are relevant and actionable to people throughout the organization is equally important. It cannot be done by hoping it will happen, saying a group prayer at the quarterly partner meeting or with a few PowerPoint slides at an all staff meeting. Firms that realize the benefits from the model the quickest are those who develop written Client Service Plans (CSPs) with the model at their core and:

- Have a process in place to measure client satisfaction and estimate the firm's wallet share.

- Target the right clients—those with the highest potential for additional services or who are most vulnerable to competitors.

- Select the right number of clients to prevent the process from becoming overwhelming.

- Supplement the current client-service team with industry or functional specialists to have a fresh set of ears in the room.

- Ensure the process is a client-facing interaction, not an internal paper chase.

- Act on the lessons learned from the process to enhance client service in ways that continuously demonstrate to clients that they made a good choice.

- Measure results in increased client satisfaction, client retention and wallet share, and tie some portion of incentive compensation to these vital metrics.

These firms also develop their CSPs using the same tools and techniques they deploy when courting an important prospect. This typically involves:

- A team of people from multiple disciplines.

- A considerable investment of face time by firm leaders and industry/functional experts listening to the prospects' needs.

- Educating the prospect on the firm's range of services and capabilities.

DO YOUR HOMEWORK
Most firms assume that the best targets for client service plans are their largest accounts. While we agree these clients deserve high touch and lots of love, we prefer to start the process by estimating each client's total spend on professional services, regardless of the amount the firm is actually capturing.

This information should be readily available on most clients. In those few situations when it is not, we estimate total spend based on comparably sized clients in similar industries.

We then rank clients by total spend, strategic fit and client characteristics, focusing on the top 20 or 30%. For most firms, there will be a natural break between those two data points. These are high-opportunity clients and good candidates for client service plans.

Are we ignoring the majority of a firm's other clients? Not at all. While we ensure they continue to receive great client service through client feedback assessments and meetings, they aren't CSP candidates. By focusing on clients who have a demonstrated history of significant annual spending, we can reduce the CSP candidates to a manageable number.

Armed with our list of high-opportunity clients, we add two attributes — our percentage share of each client's annual spend and the client satisfaction/loyalty score. We then group clients on a high/low scale, such as high or low wallet share, or high or low client satisfaction/loyalty. The resulting sort puts each of the high-opportunity clients in one of four categories.

Client Classifactions

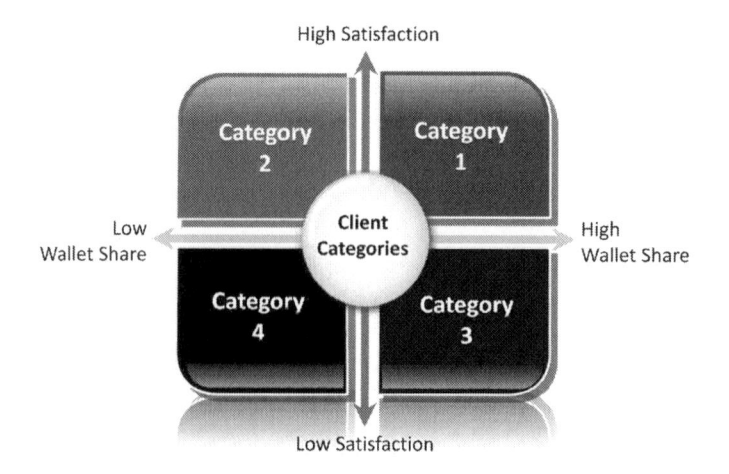

High Satisfaction

Category 2	Category 1
Category 4	Category 3

Low Wallet Share — Client Categories — High Wallet Share

Low Satisfaction

Category 1: High wallet share, high satisfaction/loyalty. Competitors covet these clients and aggressively solicit their business. Thus, the focus of the CSP with this group is client appreciation and retention. (we often call it a value review). The CSP team should meet face-to-face with the client on a regular basis to reinforce the firm's value proposition in the relationship and emphasize a commitment to excellent client service. During the session, the team should also set expectations around client service quality, response times, delivery dates and how the client wants to be served. From an operational viewpoint, there should be no question that these clients get top priority in staffing decisions and scheduling. They should also be where you look for referrals, since it's clear these clients know you, like you and trust you.

Category 2: Low wallet share, high satisfaction/loyalty. These are prime candidates for an expanded relationship and increased revenue. While they spend freely on professional services and are pleased with the firm's client service, they're not choosing the firm for the majority of their work. Based on our experience interviewing clients in this category, we find they have not been properly approached, are unaware of the breadth of services the firm offers or thinks the firm is too busy to take on more assignments. In any case, applying the full CSP process to this group can result in a sizeable return on investment. As an added benefit, note how these clients can also be rich sources of referrals.

Category 3: High wallet share, low satisfaction/loyalty: These clients should be a top priority, since they spend a sizeable percentage of their wallet with the firm, but are not happy with client service. Management should focus on meeting with these clients to ask good questions, probe for their core issue and make the necessary changes to save the relationship. That may mean changing the partner relationship, adjusting the client service team, investing time to re-engineer client service delivery, holding the team accountable for timely delivery or addressing other issues that are sources of client distress.

Category 4: Low wallet share, low satisfaction/loyalty. These clients typically share some characteristics. Realization and collected rate-per-hour is low, they challenge already discounted billings and they don't pay bills on time. Frequently, these clients cause delays in engagement wrap-up and scheduling issues, and they are often tough on staff. Firm management should assess the time and effort required to convert these problem accounts into better clients, or seriously consider the firm's risk-reward in continuing the relationship. In most cases, these are the easiest clients a firm can choose to lose.

Select the Team

Once the firm has grouped clients into categories, leaders must decide who should be on the CSP development team. Firm participants should be senior members of the client service team, which should also include an industry expert and at least one functional specialist. The client relationship partner can fill one of those roles, but not both. Involving a firm member who is well versed in overall capabilities is a plus, but make sure the firm team doesn't outnumber the client service team.

Before meeting with clients, the firm team should convene to educate all members about the client. This discussion should include reviewing results of the latest client satisfaction survey, recent financial performance, company history, industry information and issues highlighted by the client service team. It's also wise to ensure all team members are aware of any views the client may hold about professional service firms or your firm in particular. Effective preparation for a CSP meeting typically requires two to three hours from each team member.

Prior to the actual client meeting, assign key roles, which includes choosing a facilitator, timekeeper and scribe. It is vital that the relationship partner not fill any of those roles, so he or she is free to focus completely on listening to the client. The team should prepare open-ended questions that will help the client focus on specific business issues. For example, one open-ended question might be, "As you think about the future of your business and your various strategies and initiatives, what are you most excited about? Concerned about?"

Some firms attempt to charge the client for a CSP meeting. In our experience, we have found that to be a barrier. A firm wouldn't ask important prospects to pay for scoping the work and presenting a proposal. The same holds true for a client service plan. We find the time invested in these meetings typically pays for itself in additional projects from current clients.

LISTEN UP!
A CSP cannot be effective without a face-to-face client meeting. This important discussion usually takes two or three hours, and it should include all key client decision-makers, including the CEO.

Start the client meeting with brief introductions. Then, restate the meeting's primary goals, which may include a better understanding of the client, clearer direction on how to serve their needs and a stronger framework around how the client wants to be served by the firm.

Next, sit back and listen. This is the client's opportunity to talk about specific business needs, not an infomercial about your firm. Actively hearing the client's point of view is the firm team's critical role in this session.

CAPTURE THE INSIGHTS

You'll want to record the broad range of insights and learnings gained from your CSP meetings in a disciplined, structured way. This information will include:

- Client information, such as defined service priorities and who is on the client service team.

- A Client Profile, made up of key facts about the client, a snapshot of the client's industry and important historical events.

- A Relationship Map, which is a list of internal and external individuals associated with the client.

- A Strategic Profile, which is the client's perspective on its goals, plans, issues and opportunities.

- An Action Plan, made up of the specific objectives, goals, strategies and measures, as well as who is responsible/accountable for each of these areas.

On our website you'll find the CSP template that we tailor to the needs of each of our clients. In our experience, we find this structured approach ensures we ask the right questions, while making it much easier to catalog collective insights and learnings. (You can download the template at www.MoreWalletShare.com.)

This, in turn, helps us share accumulated knowledge with others, and hold both partners and staff accountable for agreed-upon strategies, tactics and measures.

Much To Gain, Little To Lose

When done properly, the CSP process has many benefits. One is how the client resells himself on the value your firm brings to his organization. We also find that the client usually identifies several new service opportunities for the firm after a CSP session and often directly ask for the firm's help during the meeting or request a proposal for specific projects.

During a CSP session that we facilitated for a firm's tax-only client, the client CFO mentioned her major project for the coming year was the implementation of an Enterprise Resource Planning system (ERP). While she was the champion of the project, she was also anxious about it because it required significant changes in their processes, was internally-focused, would consume a lot of employee time across the organization, and was a large investment. At one point she asked us if our firm managed ERP implementations for other clients. "We sure do. In fact, we have the third largest practice in this area that specializes in them."

The CFO was completely unaware of the firm's capabilities in this area and invited the firm to propose on the engagement. As a direct result of the CSP meeting, the firm won a $330,000 ERP implementation project.

This example also shows the value of a team approach to serving a client. The tax partner assigned to this client was only listening for tax-related issues, such as cost segmentation, transfer pricing, and tax credits and incentives. By being focused on his own area of expertise, he completely missed a very large engagement that was about to be awarded to a competitor.

During the CSP process, clients will re-establish how they want to be served. Remember, service attributes go beyond technical expertise. These attributes include the soft aspects of client service, such as frequency and nature of contact, the makeup of the client service team, how firm personnel interact with client staff, and client expectations about response time and delivery dates. These are key elements that help fuel client satisfaction and retention.

Although listening is the firm team's key role, there will be opportunities during a CSP meeting to more fully educate the client on the firm's capabilities. That's largely because the process exposes the client to firm personnel with expertise beyond that available in the immediate client service team. Another benefit of this CSP process is how we regularly see clients "resell" themselves on their CPA firm's unique value proposition.

FOLLOW UP!

A final key component of the CSP process is for the team to validate what it heard during the client meeting. Feeling heard and understood is a critical contributor to high client satisfaction. We recommend sending a follow-up letter to the client that documents important client takeaways, key service attributes the firm will pursue and a summary of other commitments made during the meeting.

Key Learnings

- The process of developing CSPs improves relationships between partners, staff and clients. It also broadens understanding between the firm and clients and helps everyone be more effective in their jobs.

- There are five distinct stages of developing a Client Service Plan:

> Select Client & Team → Begin to Complete CSP Template → Meet with Client → Re-group and Finish the CSP → Share Final CSP with Client

- By asking each partner to develop two or three CSPs annually, over a three-year period most firms find they have prepared plans for clients that account for 80% of their revenue.

- The CSP is a great way to build client loyalty by delivering unexpected value that doesn't show up on a bill.

- The CSP for an important client is a valuable use of non-billable time.

Wallet Share Ideas to Try in Our Firm

Barriers to Implementation

Chapter 6

3x3x3℠ Accountability

"He that is good for making excuses is seldom good for anything else."
—Benjamin Franklin

We have explained the process and benefits of our 3x3x3℠ model and how it creates sticky clients and increases wallet share. You can improve client retention and grow revenue through client prioritization, better understand your clients and lost accounts through feedback, and leverage the 3x3x3℠ client service model and follow-on service plans to build unrivaled client loyalty.

But here's a cautionary note. Without a system of accountability, all of the above can be a waste of time.

We interact with hundreds of CPA firm partners each year and nearly all agree that accountability is necessary – for everyone else. For that reason, the pursuit of accountability, doing what you said you would do, to the best of your ability, without any reminders, is one of the most challenging tasks facing any CPA firm.

If your firm currently does not have a system for monitoring and enforcing accountability, we recommend you work to implement a basic system before attempting to implement the process outlined in this book. For those who do have accountability systems in place and who wish to implement the 3x3x3[SM] process, we have a question: "What are you going to stop doing to create capacity for this new activity?"

Our system has proven results. In our experience, a firm can grow revenue and profits by 10% or more using the 3x3x3[SM] model. This is in addition to the growth that comes from prospecting for new clients and referrals that come from your best promoters. But it requires partner time, consistent effort and a system of accountability that has direct linkage to a partner's compensation. We should also note that we are not suggesting firms stop prospecting or adding new clients. We are advocating for striking a better balance between growth from new clients and by expanding the services sold to existing clients.

Attributes of System for Accountability

What does a sound partner accountability and compensation system look like? Our belief is that all clients of a CPA firm are a firm asset, not a partner asset. Based on our experience managing CPA practices of all sizes, a firm partner has up to six key accountabilities that should be linked to compensation:

1. Client service excellence
    a. Develop and maintain expertise in a service or industry.
    b. Retain clients by diagnosing needs and either deliver appropriate services within the area of expertise or facilitate the delivery of those services through others.
2. Develop people
    a. Attract, train and retain talented people to sustain the firm.
3. Business growth
    a. Develop a personal reputation that attracts new client relationships to the firm.
    b. Promote ideas, products, services and solutions that result in expanded services to existing clients.
4. Leadership
    a. Demonstrate leadership within the firm, profession and local community.
    b. Demonstrate "firm first, self second" behaviors.
5. Practice management
    a. Responsibly manage the firm's assets, including realization, billing and expense control.
    b. Achieve personal productivity and appropriately utilize other resources, including utilization, collected rate and leveraging work down.
6. Compliance with quality standards set by the firm.

With these key accountabilities in mind, an effective compensation system would reward a partner for his or her personal achievements in these categories. Period. Pay for performance, not rhetoric or longevity.

Note how the size of a partner's book is not one of the factors. In our world, size does not matter, but balance does. Far too often we've seen a partner who leverages a huge book of business to create "partner centric" clients instead of "firm centric" clients. A better way is for that partner to transition clients to others, which frees up time for new business prospecting and development. Bottom-line: We believe compensation should not be based on the size of a partner's book, and the system should actually penalize a partner if there is evidence of hoarding accounts.

Similarly, partners who pound their chest about their personal charge hours do not impress us. Usually, this is another sign of hoarding work when others could be doing similar activity at a lower rate and higher realization. Typically, the partners who do not leverage down work are extremely controlling and often drive staff out of the firm, if not the profession as a whole.

We are also unimpressed with "sales superstars," particularly when they routinely bring in significant new client revenue, only to lose those same clients in a year or two because of poor client service or an unwillingness to transition the relationship to a partner with more time to focus on the accounts. If sales superstars are also the kings of revolving door clients, they are damaging your firm and brand.

In our opinion, growing the firm through expanded services is one of nine factors by which you evaluate a partner's performance. Therefore, to be effective, a firm should plan for up to 10% of an individual partner's time as non-billable in pursuit of this objective.

MEASURING WALLET SHARE

To drive accountability with our system, a firm must first establish a baseline that is used to judge the individual partner's performance in the Categories 1b and 3b above. By establishing a baseline and monitoring subsequent changes via client surveys and meetings and "wallet share" measures, the firm has a sound foundation on which to evaluate a partner's performance in those categories.

The Wallet Share Index®, expressed as a percentage, would be:

(Client's annual spend with your firm) ÷
(Client's annual spend with all firms)

However, most firms cannot produce with certainty the approximate annual spend by clients. So we prefer to use the following Wallet Share Index:

(Client's annual spend with your firm for non-traditional services) ÷ (Client's annual spend on traditional audit, bookkeeping, tax return preparation services)

Let's look at an example. Joe, an audit partner, has been assigned a $1,500,000 book of business, of which $1,000,000 was transitioned by retiring partners and $500,000 was gained through Joe's business development efforts. The mix of services within Joe's assigned clients is:

- $1,100,000 of audit and review services

- $200,000 of tax compliance

- $100,000 of tax consulting

- $100,000 of management consulting

Joe's client base is predominantly manufacturers, who are frequent buyers of value-added consulting services. Based on market research, the typical client in Joe's client base buys $1 of consulting services, with heavy emphasis in the tax area, for every $1 of traditional compliance services.

Based on that analysis, it's clear Joe is not capitalizing on the potential $1,300,000 of extended services within his assigned client base. However, we recognize that Joe's firm cannot provide all of the extended services his clients routinely buy. That means we're looking for incremental improvement, not miracles.

Joe's wallet share index (the percentage of extended services to compliance services) is $200,000 extended/$1,300,000 compliance. That works out to 15%. Given his client base, which spends $1 in extended for every $1 of compliance, Joe should have a partner scorecard that puts heavy emphasis on improving his wallet share index. By using the 3x3x3^{SM} model to introduce others (especially those with strong tax background) into the client relationship, Joe could capture some of that wallet share. Here's how:

Suppose Joe agrees to a goal of increasing his wallet share index from 15 to 20% (a small increment). The following year, Joe achieves the following:

- $1,160,000 of audit (all due to fee increases on his $1,100,00 base)

- $220,000 of tax compliance (fee increase on his $200,000 base)

- $260,000 of tax consulting (a $150,000 increase, all identified, scoped and sold by others on the team with tax expertise)

- $110,000 of management consulting (increase due to fee increases)

In this example, Joe's managed revenue grew from $1,500,000 to $1,750,000 (a 17% increase without picking up a single new client). Meanwhile, his wallet share index improved from 15% to 27%. Most, if not all, of this increase will flow directly to the bottom line, since it's unlikely Joe's firm will add staff to handle the incremental work.

Multiply Joe's results across the rest of the firm's partners and you begin to realize the impact of mining current clients for additional opportunities. But these gains can only happen if you hold partners accountable for implementing the 3x3x3^{SM} process.

Consider a more broad-scale example, in which the firm puts our entire system to work. In this scenario, imagine Joe leveraging "clients willing to refer" who were discovered through a client survey (Chapter 2). These referrals led to two new clients, producing first-year revenue of $100,000. This means Joe's assigned clients now grew from $1,500,000 to $1,850,000, or a 23% one-year increase. That's before we include Joe's business development efforts outside his client base.

Key Learnings

- To successfully utilize the process and behavior changes in this book that lead to sticky clients, a firm has to establish accountability as a core value.

- The compensation system needs to reward partners for exhibiting desired behaviors and achieving specific objectives related to accountability. New metrics, such as the Wallet Share Index, need to be adopted and tracked.

Wallet Share

Wallet Share Ideas to Try in Our Firm

Barriers to Implementation

CHAPTER 7

Building On the 3x3x3[SM] Model

"When a great team loses through complacency, it will constantly search for new and more intricate explanations to explain away defeat."
—*Pat Riley*

Understanding client perceptions is just one step in building a sustainable CPA firm practice. There are two other constituencies whose insights and perspectives need to be regularly assessed: staff/employees and partners/owners. By gauging perceptions in all three areas, you'll have the deepest understanding of how the firm is perceived and the most accurate view of how these important stakeholder interests are aligned. Armed with this information, you can confidently build relevant, actionable plans to serve, retain and grow clients (and staff), all while improving the odds of taking your firm to the next level.

A CPA firm's two most important assets are its clients and staff. Generally, there are four basic firm activities that are common to both: attract, secure, engage and keep engaged.

Ironically, the failings of both relationships tend to occur for similar reasons. Firms typically do a great job with prospects and candidates in the first two areas (attract and secure), but then something happens. Firms often stop investing the time necessary to engage, and keep engaged, these vital assets. It's as if we forget that, with little or no notice, a key client contact can change jobs or a staff person can leave your firm. In all cases, they will remember the relationship with your firm and carry forward those impressions.

Last, we regularly see an internal battle about which is more important, clients or staff. As Teresa Hopke, Senior Vice President with the workforce strategy consultancy Life Meets Work, Inc., has pointed out to us, "…(firms) should stop trying to weigh one over the other and understand that they are equally important. You can't have one without the other."

To Retain Staff, Engage Them

Retaining a firm's top talent is among the biggest concerns of CPA firm leaders. For example, our 2013 Growth Prospects Survey showed that 62% of firm leaders are concerned or very concerned about retaining top talent. Perhaps it's driven by the equally high degree of concern about replacing top talent when it leaves the organization.

The key to retaining staff is commonly referred to as "employee engagement," and many of its concepts can also be applied to clients. In the past, employee engagement was less of an issue, as there seemed to be an unwritten loyalty pact between employers and employees: do good work and continuously add value and there will be a place for you in the firm. The era of being with one company from "womb to tomb" is gone, as is the expectation of receiving a gold watch and a pension in return for many years of service. Those notions of loyalty have been replaced by the expectation that staff should be committed and engaged while working for the firm.

What is Employee Engagement?

Employee engagement is defined as the emotional commitment a person has to the firm and its goals. It is what motivates people to willingly exert discretionary effort without being told, asked or watched. Individuals don't make the effort because they'll get paid for it or because it will lead to a promotion. Engagement is, for example…

- What motivates the second-year staff person to put in overtime without being asked

- What motivates the IT Help Desk coordinator to come to your office to install a print driver on your laptop even though she has her coat on and is just about to leave the office for the weekend

- What motivates the manager to volunteer to represent the firm at a college recruiting event even though a partner won't be present

Like client loyalty, improvements to employee engagement should not be limited to increased happiness or satisfaction. These set the bar too low. Happy and satisfied employees may show up to work without complaints, but being happy or satisfied doesn't necessarily mean they're productive, working toward critical firm goals or not listening to recruiters who offer them a sizable pay increase.

How Engaged Employees Add Value

There's ample evidence available that shows a direct correlation between firm performance and employee engagement. For example, as Kevin Kruse points out in his book Employee Engagement 2.0, engaged employees work harder, longer and with more focus. That can lead to:

- Higher service, quality and productivity, which leads to…

- Higher client satisfaction, which leads to…

- Higher revenue (using more services and referrals), which leads to…

- Higher levels of profit, which leads to…

- Higher shareholder returns (i.e., partner comp)

How can an engaged employee add value to the firm? Why should you be making investments in developing engaged employees? Which of these scenarios would you prefer?

- An In-Charge on one of your long-term clients is doing the minimum necessary to get by. It takes him about a week to respond to e-mails and phone messages from the client, he's sent the client several reports that had to be recalled to correct obvious errors that he missed when he proofed them, and he regularly shows up 5 to 10 minutes late for team meetings.

- A manager who works with one of your larger clients is enthusiastic and eager to solve the client's problems. Just last week she showed them a way they could reduce their taxes by $45,000 by taking advantage of a little known incentive that's available from the state. Earlier in the year, on her way home after work on a Friday night, she drove about 25 minutes out of her way to drop off a set of financial statements she knew the CFO would probably need for an important meeting that weekend. And, she's referred a couple of the firm's other clients to her client, which led to an incremental $175,000 of business for the latter.

Investing in the development and growth of your people is one way to demonstrate you value them. As Teresa Hopke at Life Meets Work, Inc. has also pointed out to us, most firms make a disproportionate investment in their client service tools compared to developing the soft skills of their people. "There seems to be an assumption in many firms that people are skilled at that out of the womb or they will somehow magically acquire the (non-technical) skills they need to create sticky clients as they move up the ranks. In reality, those skills need to be developed in the same way technical competence was developed."

Partner/Owner Perceptions

Alignment among firm partners/owners should not be assumed. Such alignment frequently depends on the issue and can last anywhere from a few days to many years through successive managing partners. Like the wheels on a car, maintaining alignment requires care, preventative action and regular check-ups. By the time you can see the effects of mal-alignment, the remedy is usually costly, time consuming and not much fun.

A formal assessment of how the firm's partners/owners perceive internal/external opportunities and challenges should be done on a regular basis. A good time for such an assessment would either be before the annual partner meeting or prior to development of the annual operating plan. In this assessment, it's important to understand both the degree of concern about issues (from

Extremely Concerned to No Concern At All) and the relative importance of each issue to the firm (from High to Low). Topic areas to cover would include:

- Firm governance
- Partner compensation
- Growth
- Profitability
- Staff
- Clients
- Competition
- Environment (regulatory, economy, etc.)

By using a repeatable, disciplined process for these assessments, it's easy to compare results among functions, between equity and income partners, among offices and over time. It will allow you to identify areas of consensus, chart obstacles to progress and gain insight on how to allocate resources to support growth, profitability, innovation (e.g. developing new products and services), differentiation (e.g., strengthening an existing expertise), collaboration (e.g., modifying the comp plan to encourage multi-function pursuit teams), and process improvement (e.g., establishing a reverse mentoring program) initiatives.

LEVERAGING ALL THE FEEDBACK YOU'VE GATHERED
Collecting insights from clients, staff and partners need not be a daunting, time-consuming task. It can

be done with a combination of internal resources and independent third parties, and spread throughout the year. The hardest part is getting started, but once the processes become part of the way you do business, the amount of time and investment quickly diminishes. While gathering feedback from clients, staff and partners requires a substantial commitment, sharing the learnings up, down and across the firm is what ensures there's a return on your investment.

For example, to be fully engaged, staff want to know how they can contribute to the success of the firm. Sharing with them the key drivers for retaining clients will help them anticipate the unmet and emerging needs of their clients, and meet or exceed their expectations. They'll be able to adjust their priorities so they are focused on what's most important without continuous partner or client oversight.

Another way to use the new insights and learnings is to prepare a SWOT Analysis (Strengths, Weaknesses, Opportunities, Threats) for the firm. It will help guide preparation of strategic and annual operating plans. Below is the SWOT template we use with clients that can be downloaded at www.MoreWalletShare.com.

SWOT Analysis

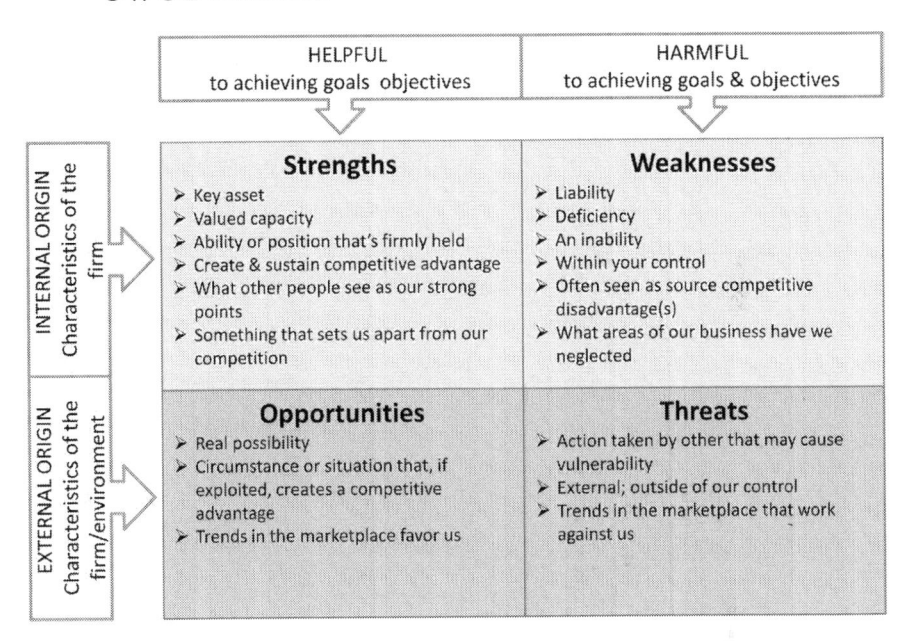

	HELPFUL to achieving goals objectives	HARMFUL to achieving goals & objectives
INTERNAL ORIGIN Characteristics of the firm	**Strengths** ➢ Key asset ➢ Valued capacity ➢ Ability or position that's firmly held ➢ Create & sustain competitive advantage ➢ What other people see as our strong points ➢ Something that sets us apart from our competition	**Weaknesses** ➢ Liability ➢ Deficiency ➢ An inability ➢ Within your control ➢ Often seen as source competitive disadvantage(s) ➢ What areas of our business have we neglected
EXTERNAL ORIGIN Characteristics of the firm/environment	**Opportunities** ➢ Real possibility ➢ Circumstance or situation that, if exploited, creates a competitive advantage ➢ Trends in the marketplace favor us	**Threats** ➢ Action taken by other that may cause vulnerability ➢ External; outside of our control ➢ Trends in the marketplace that work against us

If you're contemplating a departure from the firm, or putting out feelers with strategic buyers, the insights you gain from client, staff and partner research can help you proactively close gaps and increase the firm's value to a potential suitor.

If you're integrating a new firm into your business, gathering feedback from both organizations will allow you to uncover land mines, leverage areas of agreement and score some immediate "wins" with clients and staff.

The learnings from clients and staff can be used in your recruiting literature, on your website, and in proposals to help differentiate you from competitors. If you participate in any of the "best places to work" surveys, the insights you'll gain from this stakeholder research will help you make the cut. The mere fact that you solicit feedback from these groups on a regular, systematic basis should improve your position on most of these lists.

KEY LEARNINGS

- Continuously improving employee engagement is a proven strategy for retaining staff and clients.

- Investing in the development of the soft skills of your staff is one way to show people that you care about them and engage them, and the skills they learn can be the difference between mediocre and rock star client service.

- Integrating the insights of clients, staff, and partners/owners into overall firm planning increases its relevance, catalyzes the ability to gain support and enhances the likelihood plans will deliver the intended results.

- Firm leadership needs to focus on using the learnings and insights gathered from clients, staff and partners to drive action, change and results.

Wallet Share Ideas to Try in Our Firm

Barriers to Implementation

Closing Thoughts

*"The first sign we don't know what we are doing
is an obsession with numbers."*
—*Johann Wolfgang von Goethe*

How often have you sat through a partner meeting or annual retreat where reams of financial data are reviewed: revenue, charge hours, collected rate, realization, utilization, etc.? Many firms seem to review everything on the income statement and balance sheet as if the components were equally important, and they do it with the granularity of an electron microscope and the precision of an atomic clock.

While firm financials are important, they are but one scorecard. Those numbers, by themselves, do not provide insights into the story behind them. To understand what led to the numbers, time needs to be spent discussing the firm's two most important assets: its people and its clients. For example…

- Recent proposal wins and losses
- Client departures and client retention rates
- Top client "touches" per month
- Voluntary staff turnover
- Latest Net Promoter Scores
- Changes in Wallet Share Index
- Identification of key strategic hires and status of filling open positions
- Insights from client satisfaction/loyalty surveys
- Updates on improving staff engagement

We find that when time is taken to get behind the numbers there's almost always a story that involves clients and/or staff. Common themes include:

- Meeting or not meeting emerging needs
- Services that are no longer relevant or less valued
- Competitors luring away clients/staff
- Feelings of being appreciated/valued or ignored/taken for granted
- Exceeding or failing to meet expectations and commitments
- Environmental changes that are outside of our control
- Lack of responsiveness or anticipating a client's needs

Closing Thoughts

- Assigning either the best or a sub-optimal team to clients
- Greed, arrogance and/or complacency

We believe that by striving to make clients sticky, many of the themes above are proactively addressed or avoided altogether. The result is clients loyal to the firm and greater wallet share. This loyalty leads to sustainable practices that are not dependent on one partner, a lone contact or a single service. Loyal clients are more profitable because they use multiple services, understand the difference between value and price, and are very likely to be ambassadors for your firm.

Daniel Pink, in his 2012 book To Sell is Human, captures the essence of what we are advocating throughout this book. He notes that to be successful at what we do, we have "…to help others see their situations in fresh and more revealing ways and to identify problems they didn't realize they had."

The 3x3x3℠ Model is a process for securing, retaining and growing clients. The process of creating sticky clients enables you to unlock the hidden wealth in your existing book of business, which can drive dramatic growth and value. When the tools and processes we've described throughout this book are implemented, it creates competitive advantage, because the 3x3x3℠ Model makes it harder for clients to leave your firm for a competitor. Based on our first hand experience, we have found this to be the case. We hope you will too.

About L. Harris Partners

Managing partners, practice leaders, and department heads who want to grow their professional service firms know that tapping into the expertise of those who have successfully navigated the same terrain gives them an advantage. L. Harris Partners is who they turn to for the expertise and advice to increase wallet share, grow revenue and enhance firm value.

L. Harris Partners is comprised of professional service firm veterans with C-level executive experience who've walked in the shoes of managing partners as well as in those of their clients. They have worked in multiple functions, in multiple industries and internationally. They've developed and proven their processes in the field, and generated game-changing results.

L. Harris Partners brings recent, relevant and hands-on experience to its clients and projects because its professionals...

- See big-picture trends and themes

- Have actually managed practices, niches and service lines of all sizes

- Put process and discipline around what matters most

- Ask the questions that a firm can't ask or doesn't know to ask

- Make practical recommendations that can actually be implemented

- Know how to execute plans and hold people accountable for their commitments

When you've tried to solve an important problem twice and haven't gotten the results you need or expect, consider calling L. Harris Partners.

www.LHarrisPartners.com
(312) 775-4055 (Chicago)
(952) 944-3303 (Minneapolis)

Made in the USA
Charleston, SC
14 June 2013